Ben Simmons: The Inspiring Story of One of Basketball's Rising All-Stars

An Unauthorized Biography

By: Clayton Geoffreys

Table of Contents

Foreword

Whenever you are selected at the top of your class, the bar gets set high. Ben Simmons' selection as the top overall pick in the 2016 NBA Draft was no exception. Unfortunately for him, his first year in the league was marred by a broken right foot. That setback has long been forgotten since. Debuting for his rookie season in the 2017-2018 season, Ben Simmons began his journey proving his doubters wrong and solidifying himself as one of the league's immediate stars to watch. In 2019, his abilities were validated as he was selected for his first NBA All-Star selection. Ben Simmons still has a lot to look forward to in his career. After all, at the time of this writing, he is just twenty-two years old. His prime is still ahead of him and he has so much more to continue to grow in to become one of the league's next unforgettable stars. Thank you for purchasing *Ben Simmons: The Inspiring Story of One of Basketball's Rising All-Stars*. In this unauthorized biography, we will learn Ben Simmons' incredible life story and impact on the game of basketball. Hope you enjoy and if you do, please do not forget to leave a review!

Also, check out my website at claytongeoffreys.com to join my exclusive list where I let you know about my latest books. To thank you for your purchase, you can go to my site to download a free copy of *33 Life Lessons: Success Principles, Career Advice & Habits of Successful People*. In the book, you'll learn from some of the greatest thought leaders of different industries on what it takes to become successful and how to live a great life.

Cheers,

Clayton Geoffreys

Visit me at www.claytongeoffreys.com

Introduction

Traditionally, basketball players have always been defined by their size. The bigger and taller the player is, the bigger his position was. Players 6'9" or taller would usually play the power forward and center positions. And naturally, smaller players usually play either guard positions. This has been the case since basketball was first invented. Those who are taller have the natural advantage near the basket while those who are shorter are usually quicker and more mobile than other players.

However, over the last handful of decades, the NBA has seen its share of generational talents that play entirely different styles than what people would expect based on their size. You see players that look like they play the forward positions playing guard. And there are those that are listed as wing players who act more like playmakers whenever they are on the floor.

Considered as "big guards," these players may look like your conventional forwards or wings but have the skill set of point guards. They run like guards, handle the ball like playmakers, and run plays for the entire team like they are six feet tall. Using their superior size, such players have become matchup nightmares in the NBA.

Considered the very first big guard, Oscar Robertson had the size of a wing player back in the '60s and early '70s but played more like a point guard. Using his size, he could bully his way to the basket, score over the top of the defense, rebound at a high rate, and make plays for his teammates. That is why Oscar Robertson was the first and only player in more than five decades to average a triple-double.

During the '80s, we saw the arrival of Earvin "Magic" Johnson. At almost 6'9", he was basically as big as a power forward but had the skills of an all-time great point guard. Because he was basically a head taller than all of his matchups but just as mobile as any other point guard, it was easy for him to see over the top of the defense and get from one point to another to make plays at a high rate for his teammates.

Magic paved the way for a new breed of playmakers as his all-around skills allowed him to do whatever he wanted to do on the floor while leading the Los Angeles Lakers to five championships during the '80s. As such, everyone wanted to be like Magic Johnson and several more players started to follow in his footsteps.

And during the 2000s, LeBron James burst into the scenes as an ultra-athletic small forward with the size and strength of a power forward but the skills of a playmaker. Though he was listed as a small forward, LeBron was always his team's de facto point guard. Many would argue that he was his generation's version of Oscar Robertson and Magic Johnson rolled into one.

But LeBron James' era is beginning to see its twilight years, and the NBA is now in the middle of a drastic evolution as more and more stars are now playing styles that are completely different than what their size would suggest. Called "unicorns," these are players that have the size and length of power forwards or centers but the skills of guards. And one of the more remarkable unicorns in today's era is Ben Simmons.

At 6'10" and with a mature muscular frame, Ben Simmons looks like your normal power forward. He even is big enough to play the center position in today's modern NBA. However, what surprises everyone is that he is a point guard. Simmons has the athletic ability and mobility of an All-Star wing player and the size of a big man but is a playmaker who can pass and handle the ball better than most point guards.

Growing up in Australia, the young Ben Simmons already showed enough promise for him to get a lot of attention in the United States. But when he felt like the competition in Australia was not enough for him, he moved to the United States to play high school and college basketball there. And even in the US, he was better than his peers primarily because he was playing as a power forward with the skills of a point guard.

As Ben Simmons toyed with the competition he faced in high school and college, his all-around play at his height and frame had coaches and basketball experts thinking that he could be the next coming of LeBron James or Magic Johnson. Simmons was becoming so good and versatile that he was drawing comparisons to some of the greatest players the game has ever seen. As such, there was no argument that he was going to be the top overall pick of the 2016 NBA Draft.

In 2016, what everyone expected came true when the Philadelphia 76ers went on to select Ben Simmons with the first overall pick of the draft. He was the player they thought would finally complete "the process," which was the Philadelphia 76ers' long-term rebuilding efforts that started several seasons before Simmons was drafted. He had enough talent in him to make the Sixers believe that the franchise was finally going to make a quick turnaround after years of toiling as bottom-feeders in the NBA.

However, Ben Simmons suffered a foot injury during training camp. The injury left him out of the lineup for the entire season and Simmons failed to suit up for the Sixers in what was supposed to be his rookie season. Nevertheless, he used that time off to improve his game and better prepare himself for the rigors of the NBA.

After a year of training, Ben Simmons came back healthy and better than ever. He had improved himself so much during that one-season break that he convinced the Philadelphia 76ers coaching staff that he was going to be their point guard of the future. After spending the majority of his playing years as a forward, Simmons made a smooth transition to a point guard in the NBA. And at 6'10", he became the tallest point guard in league history.

While many thought he would struggle as a full-time point guard because he did not have the shooting touch required of today's modern-day playmakers, Ben Simmons silenced his doubters. Using his size to his advantage, he could bully anyone smaller than him. And when teams decided to put bigger players on him, Simmons used his superior speed and mobility to get to the basket with ease.

At his size, it also was very easy for Ben Simmons to see over the top of the defense to make passes only he could hit with so much accuracy. The way he broke defenses down and quarterbacked his team's offense using his all-around skills at his size was something no other 6'10" player has ever done in the history of the league. He was the calming presence that gave the Sixers stability as the franchise fast-tracked "the process" and finally broke their playoff drought.

But Simmons, as a point guard, was not all about passing. Because of his size, mobility, and freakish athletic abilities, Simmons is like a freight train when he is making his way to the basket. He is unstoppable during transition and is one of the best in the NBA when it comes to finishing plays near the rim. Defenses are even so afraid of his drives to the basket that they would rather sag off and dare him to shoot jumpers. But that was never enough to truly stop him.

After averaging numbers close to a triple-double in only his first season as an NBA player, Ben Simmons was named Rookie of the Year in a close battle against the equally sensational Utah Jazz guard Donovan Mitchell. And less than a year after getting named Rookie of the Year, Simmons was named an All-Star in only his second season in the NBA.

Still very young, Ben Simmons has already created a new breed of point guards in an entirely different NBA landscape that is still very much evolving. A man at his size should not even be able to move and handle and pass the ball like a point guard, but Simmons does it at a level that is on par with some of the greatest that have ever played the game.

When all is said and done, we might even see Simmons' name up there with some of the best players the league has ever seen. But as of now, he is still on his way to greater things as he continues to help lead the Philadelphia 76ers back to the franchise' glory days. And while he does so, Simmons could also be one of the NBA's poster boys for years to come.

Chapter 1: Childhood and Early Days

Benjamin David Simmons was born on July 20, 1996, in Melbourne, Australia to parents Dave and Julie Simmons. Julie was born Australian and was previously married before meeting Dave. She was a divorced single mother of four children before she met Dave Simmons back in 1991 and before having Ben and his sister.

Meanwhile, David "Dave" Simmons was born American and is a native of New York City. At 6'9", Dave Simmons played basketball at a high level and was a power forward and center on the teams he played for. He was a standout in South Bronx High School before moving on to play college basketball at Oklahoma City University.

Dave Simmons graduated from Oklahoma City and played for a few small teams all over Central and South America. Then in 1989, after getting an offer to move to Australia, the elder Simmons decided to pack his bags and signed a contract to play for the Melbourne Tigers of the Australian National Basketball League. It was there in Australia where he became a star basketball player.

In just his first season in Australia, Dave Simmons became a fan favorite and was regularly putting up 20 points a night while grabbing rebounds in bunches as a dominant big man. He even led the Melbourne Tigers to the NBL postseason for the first time in franchise history in just his first year with the team. Then, a year later, he was one of the biggest reasons for the Tigers' NBL championship run.

It was during his time with the Melbourne Tigers that Dave met Julie, his wife-to-be. The two got married in 1994 as Dave juggled stints with the Melbourne Tigers and Westchester Stallions in the United States Basketball League back in the US. Then, in 1996, the couple's union bore Benjamin Simmons.

Throughout Ben Simmons' early life as a toddler, Dave continued his professional basketball career in Australia. He had short stints with the Newcastle Falcons, Sydney Kings, and Rockhampton Rockets over at the Queensland Basketball Team. And in 1999, Dave became a naturalized Australian citizen and joined the Canberra Cannons for two seasons before retiring as a basketball player, though he still spent time with the Hunter Pirates as an assistant.

Though Ben Simmons was too young at that time, he still spent much of his childhood days watching his father playing professional basketball during the latter's twilight years. At that time, he was raised in Newcastle when Dave was still a player for the Newcastle Falcons. It was through his father that Ben learned to play and love basketball. And because of Dave's natural athleticism and talents for the sport, Ben was seemingly born with the potential as a future basketball player himself.

Dave Simmons noticed that his son was progressing early. Ben could already run shortly after his first birthday.[i] That was what prompted the older Simmons to put his son in basketball clinics at an early age. By the time he was five years old, Ben Simmons was already practicing with 12-year-old basketball prospects in Australia because he was already physically ready to play with them.

However, Ben Simmons originally did not like playing basketball. He was a shy boy that was afraid to show what he could do in front of kids much older than he was. But his mother had to bribe him. With Ben sitting on the bench, Julie told him that she would give him a hundred dollars if he played. And once Simmons started playing, the nerves gradually started to fade away.[i]

Ben Simmons displayed his basketball talents early in his life as he was exposed to the game earlier than most kids. He was only seven years old when he began to play organized basketball and was a member of the Newcastle Hunter's under-12 team. Over the next three years, he shuffled time between his teams in Lake Macquarie and Newcastle.[ii] At that time, Ben was also a two-sport athlete and spent time playing for local rugby teams as well.

After three seasons playing under-12 basketball and rugby in Newcastle, where he was raised during his early years, Ben Simmons moved back with his family to Melbourne after his father retired as a professional basketball player. In Melbourne, he continued to play basketball and played for the junior team of the Knox Raiders.

Because of his experience in rugby, Ben Simmons also excelled in Australian Rules football in Melbourne. He was a consistent standout as a football player and played for the Beverley Hills Junior Football Club. He even won the Best and Fairest Award, which was their version of the MVP, in the Yarra Junior Football League when he was just 14 years old.[iii]

Back when he was playing basketball and Aussie football, Ben Simmons was already considered an athletic freak. He was taller and bigger than most kids his size but he moved like he was a young kid a foot shorter than he was. Professionals and teammates alike were amazed and astounded at how mobile and athletic he already was. Simmons was a kid that could jump high and run hard. And had he stuck with football, he might have even been one of Australia's premier players.[ii]

Australian Rules football was played a lot differently compared to American football or soccer. Players advance the ball up the field by running with the ball in their hands and pass it using hand passes (or by punching the ball over to another player) or by kicking it. A player with the ball needs to pass it to a teammate every 15 meters to make sure his team maintains possession of it.

In a lot of ways, Aussie football was a lot like a hybrid of American football and soccer in the sense that you need to constantly pass the ball and you can tackle other players as well. And of course, goals are scored by kicking the ball through the goal. It was a sport that was entirely different from basketball, which was Ben Simmons' other sport at that time.

Although Aussie rules football was played in an entirely different way compared to basketball because the skills needed for either sport did not mirror each other, it still helped Ben Simmons develop into the player he needed to be to excel in hoops. The football he played back then helped develop his instincts and the physicality he brought with him to basketball.

Australian NBA player Joe Ingles, who also played Aussie rules football as a young boy in Australia, is one of the toughest wing players in the league today.

He might not look like he has the physique of a tough defender, but he has always been a scrapper and someone who was not afraid to take the contact on both offense and defense. He is a player that any team would love to have because of his heart and hustle. And in Ingles' mind, he believes that playing Aussie rules football helped develop in him a mindset of not being afraid of contact and physicality.

Andrew Bogut, the first Melbourne-born player to be drafted first overall in the NBA, agrees to a certain extent. In Australian Rules football, you need to learn how to create space with the area between your shoulder and elbows by constantly wrestling with opponents. And when playing that sport, Bogut says that you should also learn how to get short openings using contact.

Ben Simmons grew up as a player with that kind of a mindset. He was not afraid of the contact when playing basketball because he knew how to take it in

Australian Rules football. And of course, he was a young teenager that knew how to get to the basket to score points with ease because he could create short openings when making contact with his defenders. Those skills helped him win the MVP award when he was in the seventh grade while attending Whitefriars College.

During his early teenage years, Ben Simmons equally loved Aussie football as much as he did basketball. However, he had to make a decision between the two sports he loved playing. Luckily for the world of basketball, it was something as simple as a coach's decision that allowed Simmons to decide that he needed to focus on hoops instead.

Ben Simmons was always the tallest kid on his Australian football teams. That was what prompted his coach to play him at the ruckman position, which was given to the tallest player on the field. But he did not like playing ruckman because he had to chase the ball

all the time instead of having a chance to score it himself. Simmons wanted to be a forward, someone who could shoot the ball for goals. That was when he felt that basketball was the better sport for him.[iv]

After deciding to focus on basketball, Simmons continued to play the sport at a high level when was a 15-year-old teenager playing for Box Hill Senior Secondary College. In 2012, he accepted a scholarship at the Australian Institute of Sport. At that time, he was the talk of the nation when it came to prodigies in basketball. The coaches at the Australian Institute of Sport were excited about having him. However, his former mentors back at Box Hill Senior Secondary College had nothing but praise for the young 15-year-old star.

Considering Ben Simmons as the best athlete he has ever coached in his life, BHSSC Coach Kevin Goorjian was excited to see how far his former player could go. He always loved how athletic and gifted

Simmons was at his size.[v] The young Simmons was already someone who could dunk the ball with ease and take the basket to the rim from the backcourt in just a few seconds.

At 15 years old, Ben Simmons was already almost 6'6" tall. While that was not a rarity for players that played the forward position in basketball, what was impressive about Simmons was that he never played like a big man until just recently. Throughout his young career as a basketball player, he approached the game from the perimeter with the mindset of a guard.

That said, Ben Simmons already had the skills one would expect a playmaker would have. He was not a good shooter, but he could force his body to the basket using his size, length, and quickness. And when he was inside the paint, Simmons could finish with the best of them or find his teammates for wide-open baskets after he broke down the defense.

At that age, Ben Simmons was still in the middle of his growth spurt. David Patrick, an assistant at Louisiana State University and a good friend of the Simmons family, remembered seeing the 15-year-old Simmons looking so awkward on the floor because of how tall and uncoordinated he seemed at first. However, after seeing him again a few months later, Patrick was surprised to see that Ben had become mobile and athletic for his height and frame. That was when he told Dave Simmons that it was a good idea to bring Ben over to the US.[iv]

Ben Simmons spent only one more year in Australia, as many basketball minds had expected. The correct path for him to take at that time was to go to the United States to play college basketball, where he could play against and alongside other players that were on par with his size, skills, and athletic gifts. But before he did so, he made waves in the international scene.

Sometime in 2012, Ben Simmons wowed Americans when he participated in the Pangos All-American camp. He had grown to a height of 6'8" and was a spectacular sight for coaches and scouts alike because of his all-around abilities at that size and age. He showed his unstoppable skills in transition and was a monster when finishing near the basket. There was no doubt that Simmons was the best player at that camp.[vi] And that was surprising because he was up against young American prospects and future NBA players Wayne Selden and Stanley Johnson.[i]

Because of his breakout performance at the Pangos Camp, Ben Simmons started to draw interest from scouts all over America. The Simmons household received calls from known prep schools in the USA because they were interested in bringing the young Ben, who was a dual citizen, over to American soil to further hone the talents that he had.

Though the Simmons family was hesitant at first because they loved being together, Dave had already decided that it was best for his son to go to the States because Ben was dominating the competition in Australia. He was not going to reach his full potential if he could not play against and alongside players that were just as athletically and physically gifted as he was.[i]

Among all of the high schools that wanted Ben Simmons on board, the family chose Montverde Academy in Florida just outside of Orlando. The reason why they chose that school was that it had a lot of international students that Ben Simmons could relate to. Other than that, their basketball program was renowned nationwide as their coach Kevin Boyle was known for helping NBA player Kyrie Irving develop into a star when he was still coaching back in New Jersey. And because Simmons loved the prospect of living in Florida because of the weather, he instantly agreed with his family's decision. Ben Simmons was on his way to America to further develop into a star.[i]

Chapter 2: High School Career in America

Ben Simmons transferred to Montverde Academy in Florida as a sophomore. That school was always one of the best at developing basketball players at the prep level. They have a lot of players that have gone on to play in the NBA. Montverde also had a reputation for bringing in international talent. In fact, Simmons had just missed future teammate Joel Embiid in Montverde after the latter moved schools a year since arriving at the United States.

However, Ben Simmons also had another fellow future NBA star as a teammate in D'Angelo Russell. Had Joel Embiid stayed with Montverde, the school would have had a trio of future NBA All-Stars leading them during the 2013 season. Nevertheless, having Simmons on board was already enough for the school and they would go on to dominate the high school ranks that year.

But before embarking on a dominant showing that season, Ben Simmons had to leave a good impression on his team first. The moment he moved to Florida to play the American brand of basketball, Simmons immediately started playing. And when he began showing what he could do, he won over his coach not only with his talents but also with the mature and humble way he carried himself.

Kevin Boyle liked how humble and respectful Ben Simmons immediately was when he first got to Montverde Academy. For Boyle, it was rare to see someone who had so much confidence but was very down to earth and unselfish. At such a young age and with the talent and potential he had, Simmons was not like most star basketball players because he never carried himself like he was bigger than everyone on the team. That made him fit in right away.

The way Ben Simmons handled himself with unselfishness was due in large part to the way he was brought up as a basketball player in Australia. He immediately noticed that in America, there was a lot of individual and selfish players early on as most high school teams loved letting their stars take over. But in Australia, everything was always team-oriented from the moment the players were first taught how to dribble. That was why Simmons did not have the air that most young high school basketball stars had. Instead, he handled himself like he was the last player on his team's bench.

Though he was hampered by a minor injury, Ben Simmons did just enough to help Montverde come back from a 16-point deficit against St. Benedict's to win the national championships. It was his putback dunk in the final minutes of the game that gave Montverde the lead for the first time in the second half. From then on, he contributed well on both ends to secure a two-point lead for his team.

The following season, Ben Simmons improved immensely after gaining some confidence in his stint with the Australian men's basketball team. He became the youngest player in Australian basketball history to be a part of the national team. He even received praise from the team's head coach, who was amazed by Ben Simmons' ability to pass the ball and create for others at his size and age.[i]

Alongside Ben Simmons on that team was Dante Exum, another Australian standout who was expected to become a high draft pick in that year's NBA draft. Exum was a childhood friend of Simmons and also has a similar athletic background in the sense that his father was an American that turned pro in Australia.

As an incoming junior, Ben Simmons was already getting scholarship offers from big-time colleges and universities in America. Those schools included LSU, Kentucky, Duke, and Kansas. And if you look at the universities that were vying for his services, it seemed like someone of his caliber was better suited to go to the more successful college programs such as Kentucky or Duke, who both have coaches that are known for developing future NBA superstars.

However, before he even started his junior season in college, Ben Simmons quickly decided to end his college recruitment. Late in 2013, he verbally committed that he was going to LSU because he felt that he was going to be most comfortable playing there.[vii] Simmons also thought that he was going to progress more like a star at LSU than in other programs though he was still thankful for the offers from all of the other colleges that were willing to take him in.

After the recruitment hype had died down, Ben Simmons went back to work. Ranked as the sixth best player of the recruitment class of 2015, Simmons was going to come out of the gates proving he had improved over the break from last season. And he was not the only one who had something to prove that year.

Teammate D'Angelo Russell, who became the second overall pick of the 2015 NBA Draft, was ready to have a breakout season as well.

Together, Ben Simmons and D'Angelo Russell gave Montverde Academy a one-two punch that nobody could stop. Ben Simmons was someone who could score on the break after rebounding the ball and was unstoppable once he got near the basket. Meanwhile, the senior Russell was their outside option because of his terrific shooting touch from distance.

Montverde Academy went undefeated heading into the High School National Tournament in New York. After beating Oak Hill Academy in the championship game, Montverde became the best high school team in the country once again. Ben Simmons finished that game with 24 points and 12 rebounds and was named tournament MVP.

After finishing his junior season averaging 18.5 points, 9.8 rebounds, and 2.7 assist, Ben Simmons was regarded as the best player of his recruitment class. At that point, there was no arguing that he had become the best high school basketball player in the country. Simmons even went on to win the MVP award at the NBPA.

If there was anything that Ben Simmons learned in his three-year high school stint in the United States, it was how to become a selfish player. It might sound surprising but being selfish was indeed a good thing for Ben Simmons to be. That was what Kevin Boyle was always telling him. Dave Simmons, his father, also wanted him to be selfish at times.

Something that Ben Simmons always lacked when he was in Australia was aggression and a selfish mindset to take over games whenever his team needed him to. Growing up in Australia did well in developing his unselfish mindset as basketball programs there were more team-oriented concerning structure. But that was not always the best mindset for a budding star player like Ben Simmons.

Dave Simmons told his son that he needed to find a balance between being selfish and unselfish. He was already exposed to the Australian style of unselfish basketball and already had an idea of what it is like playing a more star-oriented style in America. And that was the player he turned out to be in his final year in high school.

Ben Simmons only proved to become a better player during his senior year. Under his sole leadership, Montverde Academy went on to win the national championship for a third consecutive year after finishing the season with a 28-1 record. In that championship game against Oak Hill, Simmons finished with monster numbers of 20 points, 11 rebounds, and six assists even after suffering a minor injury. Naturally, he was once again named tournament MVP.

In the 29 games he played that season, Ben Simmons was an unstoppable force in the paint. He averaged 28 points, 11.9 rebounds, four assists, and 2.6 steals. By averaging nearly ten more points than he did last season, Simmons was showing that he had found the right balance between selfishness and unselfishness. On top of that, he shot over 70% from the field and nobody could contain his combination of size, length, skill, and athleticism whenever he was finishing near the basket. Simmons was named the Naismith Prep Player of the Year as well as the Gatorade National Player of the Year for 2015.

After winning three straight high school championships and many individual accolades, Ben Simmons had already secured his legacy at Montverde as one of its best products. And at that point, he was on his way to a stellar college career as the top-ranked player in his recruitment class. Simmons was finally one step closer to realizing his dream of becoming an NBA player.

Chapter 3: College Career

As promised back in 2013, Ben Simmons attended LSU for college as his recruitment class' most sought-after player. And when he arrived at Baton Rouge, it was as if he was an instant celebrity there as LSU began to build a hype that centered on his all-around skills as a future NBA star. He even garnered the attention of Shaquille O'Neal, who himself is a product of LSU.

When the season started, Ben Simmons showed why he was truly deserving of all of the attention and hype he was getting. In his first game for LSU on November 13, 2015, Simmons had 11 points, 13 rebounds, and five assists in a win over McNeese State. He followed that performance up with 22 points, nine rebounds, and six assists three days later against Kennesaw State. He then finished a 3-0 start for LSU with a monster performance against South Alabama against whom he had 23 points, 16 rebounds, three assists, and two steals.

Ben Simmons was then exposed to the entire nation as one of basketball's brightest young stars. In a nationally-televised game against Marquette on November 23, Ben Simmons finished with a phenomenal performance of 23 points, 20 rebounds, and seven assists. Although it came at a loss, there was no doubt in anyone's mind that Ben Simmons truly was a talented young prospect.

On December 2, he went for another monstrous performance. In that win over North Florida, Ben Simmons finished with 43 points, 14 rebounds, seven assists, five steals, and three blocks. He was not only filling the stat sheets, but he also made history as the first player from LSU to score that many points since Shaquille O'Neal had 43 back in December of 1991.

Ben Simmons continued his rampage over the competition. On December 19 in a win over Oral

Roberts, he had 24 points, nine rebounds, and seven assists. He followed that up with a win over the American Eagles with 23 points, five rebounds, and six assists. And on January 2, 2016, he finished a win over Vanderbilt with 36 points, 14 rebounds, and four assists.

On January 5, in a win over consistent collegiate giants Kentucky, Ben Simmons finished with 14 points and ten rebounds. He performed so well in that game that the great Magic Johnson, a player he was often compared to, said that Simmons was already the best all-around basketball player since LeBron James. Johnson also went on to say that whoever picked Simmons in the upcoming draft would have a player that could immediately make in impact.[viii]

Whether or not Magic Johnson was exaggerating due to his excitement, he was making a valid point by saying that Ben Simmons was almost as good of an all-around player as LeBron was when he came to the

NBA fresh out of high school. After all, at 6'10" and 230 pounds, Ben Simmons had the size of a prototypical power forward. However, the way he played basketball on the floor made him look like an oversized point guard because of how well he could control the tempo of the game as the primary playmaker for LSU.

Following that win against Kentucky, Ben Simmons finished a loss to Florida with 28 points, 17 rebounds, and four assists. On January 23, he then had 23 points, eight rebounds, and five assists in a win over Alabama. He continued his rampage and posted eight more double-double performances in LSU's next 11 games before the conference tournament.

Coming into the SEC Tournament with a record of 18-13, LSU was the fourth seed and were not in the best shape to come out with the conference championship. In the first game of the tournament for LSU, Simmons had 15 points and eight rebounds in a win over

Tennessee. However, a day later, he struggled from the field against Texas A&M. Simmons shot 4 out of 11 from the field and finished with only ten points in that loss.

After that loss, LSU failed to earn a bid for the NCAA Tournament as Ben Simmons' college career abruptly came to an early end. He finished his first and only season with LSU averaging 19.2 points, 11.8 rebounds, 4.8 assists, and two steals. He led his team in all major statistical categories and was practically a one-man show for LSU.

Shortly after the season ended for LSU, Ben Simmons officially put an end to his stint as an LSU Tiger after declaring for the 2016 NBA Draft. Although he failed to win any major awards or even make any noise on the national collegiate stage, there was no doubt in anyone's mind that Ben Simmons was going to be the most sought-after player of his draft class.

Chapter 4: NBA Career

Getting Drafted

Even before he announced his name for the 2016 NBA Draft, Ben Simmons was always the top player of his class. That was a title he carried ever since his junior year. However, his stock only increased when showcased what he could do against college-level competition in his lone year with the LSU Tigers. At that point, there was never even a doubt that Simmons was better than everyone in his draft class. Of course, there were good reasons for scouts and experts to think that way.

Ben Simmons was, for a lack of a better way to put it, already a freak of nature concerning his physical tools. At 6'10" and with a mature body frame that was already almost 240 pounds, Simmons already had the physical tools of a legitimate big man in the NBA. But the surprising thing was that he did not look like a power forward or center when he was out on the floor.

Despite his height, length, and body frame, Simmons can move with the grace and speed of a guard that stood six feet tall and could jump as high as any 6'6" wingman in the NBA. He is an athletic marvel that does not look or seem like a person that stands 6'10". That was how much of a freak of nature Ben Simmons already was at this size. There are only a few players in the history of the league that stood at least 6'10", but he looks so much like a guard when he is out there moving on the court.

Ben Simmons' speed and quickness were always superb.[ix] He runs the floor like a gazelle and can get from point A to point B so quickly because of his freakishly long strides. He does not even move like a bumbling athletic marvel because he knows how to control his body. It seemed like you took the speed and quickness of Chris Paul and transplanted them into the body of Lamar Odom.

But his physical tools are not the only things that are guard-like about Ben Simmons. Coming into the 2016 NBA Draft, Ben Simmons' skills resembled that of a point guard rather than the power forward position he played at Montverde and LSU. He can handle the ball like a point guard, dribble the ball in traffic with the best of them, and make the right plays that only a seasoned playmaker could.

And when Ben Simmons gets in the lane, he is nearly unstoppable as a finisher. In high school with Montverde, he was shooting over 70% from the field because of his strong ability to finish through contact using his combination of size, strength, length, and skill level. In college, he ended up shooting over 56% from the field as he brought his overall finishing abilities to a much more difficult playing field.

With his size, length, speed, athleticism, ball-handling skills, and finishing abilities, Ben Simmons was always a threat to score in transition. Whenever he got the rebound, he could go from one end to another in a hurry and no one in high school or college was big or athletic enough to keep up with him. In fact, 26% of his offensive possessions when he was in LSU came from transition plays after grabbing a defensive rebound.[ix]

During half-court sets, Ben Simmons also is not someone to take lightly. Defenses might sag off him whenever he is outside the three-point line but he can still score at will. He can bully his way to the basket because of his sheer size and explosive quickness. Whenever he is inside the paint, this left-handed player can finish well with either hand. He creates good layup attempts with acrobatic and creative finishes that he can pull off against shot-blockers. And if he cannot find a good attempt near the basket, he knows how to take the contact to fish for fouls.

Ben Simmons is also a good post player. He can take defenders to the low post with his back-to-the-basket game. Using his footwork, he can pull off smooth-looking jump hooks with either hand. He is even deadlier from the mid-post because he can either blow by his defenders with his quickness or do something creative for his teammates as a playmaker.

As impressive of a transition player and inside finisher that Ben Simmons is, what was always more impressive about him was the playmaker's skill and mentality he had. Due to his upbringing in a more team-oriented style of basketball in Australia, Ben Simmons developed an unselfish mentality that helped him make the best decisions on the floor whenever he had the ball in his hands. He always seemed to know what to do on the floor whether it was scoring the ball himself or finding an open teammate for an assist.

Speaking of assists, you will be hard-pressed to find a player as big as Ben Simmons is who has such a knack for finding open teammates. At his height, he can easily see over the top of defenses and has a floor vision terrific enough to know where everyone is. And whether it was during transition opportunities or in half-court sets, Ben Simmons' ability to handle the ball and make plays for teammates using bullet passes always seemed to make him shine even brighter than he already was.

Because of his terrific ball-handling skills and ability to pass the ball like a seasoned veteran playmaker, Ben Simmons was only the fifth player in NCAA history standing 6'9" or taller to average at least five assists per-40 minutes. And surprisingly, he is the only freshman to accomplish such a feat. That goes to show how terrific of a ball-handler Simmons is and how matured his overall decision-making already was at his age.

You can just imagine Ben Simmons making passes that players like Rajon Rondo could only make.[x] But the huge advantage he has is that he is 6'10" and could see and make passes that Rondo or any other smaller point guard can only do in their dreams.

So, if you think about it, Ben Simmons there has never been a player in the history of basketball like Ben Simmons. He has the height of Lamar Odom, the ball-handling and passing of Magic Johnson, and the strength, athleticism, and finishing ability of LeBron James. That means, on offense, there is no telling what he could do as his all-around skills at 6'10" make him perfect in the modern-day era of positionless basketball in the NBA. And that is just on offense.

Defensively, Ben Simmons has a lot of promise simply because of his size, mobility, and basketball IQ. He knows how to read defenses and passes and has a knack for anticipating plays.[ix] That helps him know where the ball is going to end up after a rebound and where opposing players are going to pass the ball to. When rebounding the ball, he does not seem to act like any other rebounder in the sense that he already moves towards the miss even before other players can tell where the ball is going to end up. It is a skill that allowed him to grab rebounds in bunches and get steals off of interceptions.

Out on the perimeter, Ben Simmons has the lateral movement and speed to keep up with smaller and quicker players. Even if his assignment is faster than him, he more than makes up for it with his length and long strides. As such, he is promising as an on-the-ball defender out on the perimeter. He is also as promising inside the paint because he is strong enough to prevent big men from pushing him. That means that he has the tools and skills that allow him to fit in today's positionless era where defenses emphasize on a lot of switches. Simply put, he can guard positions 1 to 4 and is someone who opponents cannot create mismatches with.

On top of all of that, Ben Simmons has the mentality of a star. He carries himself with so much maturity and unselfishness that you cannot expect from such a dominant player. He is also a hungry and motivated young man that knows that he could still be better than he is. He competes with so much passion and has shown tremendous ability as a winner as seen from his three consecutive national championship runs back in high school. As such, he seems older than his age would show you and his basketball IQ and mentality are well beyond his years.

However, Ben Simmons still had a few weaknesses in his game coming into the 2016 NBA Draft. The first thing that stood out among all of the weak areas in his game was his inability to hit jumpers from range. In a day and age when teams and players put a lot of emphasis on outside shooting, Simmons was someone you cannot rely on when it comes to hitting shots from the perimeter.

Though Simmons' form looks fluid enough as it does not have glaring flaws, it is the one area of his game he does not feel very comfortable with.[xi] You can see how reluctant Ben Simmons is when he is left open form the perimeter as he looks like he does not want to shoot from the outside. Because of this, it was not uncommon for Simmons to go through a few scoring droughts from time to time as teams would often just dare him to beat them with his jumper.

Ben Simmons might be a very dangerous player in transition and when he can bully his way to the basket, but there is so much he can still do if you could make people fear his jumper. His lack of an outside shot limits his ability to become an even more effective player at half-court. As such, it does not only hurt his ability to score, but also his team's spacing. That said, if he wanted to produce more for his team, his jump shot is the one dimension he needed to work on obsessively.

Whenever Ben Simmons was neutralized during half-court situations (when teams decide to take away his inside game or double him), he often looked confused and unable to do anything productive. That was why his scoring slowed down as the season progressed in his lone year with LSU. Some also pointed out the Tigers' lack of success that year was primarily because opposing teams were finding creative ways to take away Ben Simmons' ability to create for himself and for others.[ix]

Ben Simmons also does not look like a player that could contribute off the ball. This is not only because he does not have the shooting touch and willingness to shoot the ball, but also because he does not thrive well as a cutter and opportunistic scorer off the ball. This might be because he has always had the ball in his hands ever since he was in high school and was never in a system that allowed him to flourish and learn how to score without handling the ball.

And while it is not a very large concern, there are still those that question whether his ability to finish in the lane could translate to the NBA. Defenders in college were not as physically strong or capable as the ones in the NBA. Rim protectors at the pro level are also a lot more adept at defending the basket. Moreover, there might even be players that are athletic, big, and quick enough to stop Simmons in transition. But as mentioned, such concerns are not very glaring as Ben Simmons has proven himself as capable and creative of an inside scorer as any other.

Although Ben Simmons has the mentality, IQ, and skills of a point guard, he looked like he struggled as a pick-and-roll ball-handler back at LSU. The pick-and-roll is a dimension of basketball that point guards should excel at because it creates a lot of mismatches and open opportunities for scoring. However, when he was running the pick-and-roll back in college, Simmons often did not look comfortable. Nevertheless, some scouts pointed out that it might have been because of LSU's lack of spacing.[ix] But whatever the reason for that is, Ben Simmons should be able to prove himself as a good pick-and-roll player if he wants to excel as a playmaker in the NBA.

On defense, Ben Simmons does indeed have the physical tools and instincts to excel as an all-around defender. However, the problem is that he often did not look like he was interested in playing excellent defense. There were times when he would rather gamble for a steal instead of getting into a good defensive stance and position.[ix] In some instances, he looked a bit passive as a defender and did not seem like he wanted to put in the necessary effort on that end of the floor. However, things might change if he went to a team that had a defense-first mentality.

Overall, Ben Simmons is a generational talent that has the perfect blend of size, speed, strength, athleticism, and skill to play multiple positions on both ends of the floor in today's positionless style of NBA basketball. He also has the mentality, drive, and potential of a star and could be someone that could immediately make an impact on the NBA.

However, there are still a lot of areas in his game he needed to work on when he was still coming into the league in 2016. If he wanted to thrive well in an NBA style that put a lot of emphasis on floor spacing and ball and people movement, Ben Simmons needed to be someone that could score the ball from anywhere on the floor or at least be willing enough to contribute without being the primary ball-handler. On top of that, he also needed to be someone willing enough to become the excellent defender that he could potentially be.

But even with those weaknesses in his game, there was no arguing Ben Simmons' status as the favorite to be drafted first overall in the 2016 NBA Draft. Aside from already having the freakish physical tools and skills that made him a rare prospect, there were no other players that came close to his talents and potential. It was not that the class of 2016 lacked talent and potential. Simmons was simply on another level compared to his peers. As such, it was almost a foregone conclusion that Ben Simmons was going to get picked with the first overall pick.

There were some experts that believed that Ben Simmons best fit for an NBA team were the Boston Celtics because Brad Stevens is known for getting the most out of his players while hiding their weaknesses in the process. In that regard, he could have utilized Simmons' freakish talents while making sure that teams do not get to exploit his lack of shooting.

The problem was that the Boston Celtics were going to pick third overall in the NBA Draft and were not in the best position to move up the standings because they did not have the trade pieces to convince the Philadelphia 76ers to trade their top overall pick. And because the Sixers did not look like they were willing to draft lanky wing player Brandon Ingram, who was predicted to go second overall, it was almost certain that Simmons was going to be a member of the Philadelphia 76ers.

At that time, Philadelphia was probably the worst team for any player to go to if they wanted to win games. The Sixers had been languishing at the bottom of the NBA standings for almost a handful of seasons already. They did not have the most talented roster at that time and were struggling to stay healthy as a team. Moreover, their top draft picks over the past few seasons had either struggled to stay away from injury or could not live up to expectations. Even their 2014 first-round pick, Joel Embiid, had yet to suit up for the team. As such, they only won ten games out of 82 during the 2015-16 season.

Nevertheless, the Sixers had been urging people to believe in their "trust the process" mantra as they were in the middle of a long-term rebuilding process that could turn the team into instant playoff contenders and even eventually a legitimate championship squad. They had Embiid waiting in the wings ready to play his first NBA season after two years of recovering from injuries and were also about to draft Ben Simmons, who was someone ready to contribute at the NBA level.

When draft night came, the NBA's worst-kept secret was revealed as the Philadelphia 76ers picked Ben Simmons as the top overall pick of the 2016 NBA Draft. Simmons had achieved his dream of becoming an NBA player, which was something even his talented father could not do. And with Simmons in the fold, the Sixers believed that they finally had the player that could help them complete "the process."

The Injury Season

After becoming only the third player born in Melbourne, Australia to be drafted first overall pick (after Andrew Bogut and Kyrie Irving), Ben Simmons suited up for the Philadelphia 76ers' Summer League team to showcase to the world what he could do against NBA-level talent early on in his career. He was yet to turn 20 when he played during the Summer League.

In his first few Summer League games, Ben Simmons struggled as a scorer and did not perform well from the field. However, he showed flashes of greatness in all of the other areas he was expected to excel in. At the forward position, the 6'10" 19-year-old Australian native looked like an oversized point guard that could control the pace of the game.

Simmons was throwing no-look passes, dropping off dimes to teammates after destroying defensive sets, and finding open teammates for assists. Even during the Summer League, Simmons was already proving himself as the best creator and passer on a subpar Philadelphia 76ers basketball club. He could control the flow of the offense. It was not like he was forced to be a playmaker as doing things that 6'10" forwards normally should not do looked natural for him.xii

At that point, because he was so good at the role of playmaker, the hardest part for the Sixers was knowing which position he was going to play. He was already unlike any other player because his size was allowing him to play at the frontcourt and because his skills made him look like a terrific backcourt player.

His father Dave Simmons even believes that he is a forward but with the ball-handling and passing skills of a guard. He always thought of his son as a small forward and never as a guard. And there was a good reason to believe that Simmons was a forward because he always played that position and was never pegged as a guard his entire basketball career.

Back then, even Philadelphia 76ers head coach Brett Brown said that he was going to play Ben Simmons at the forward position but that he would give him the ball-handling responsibilities. He might have seen

Simmons as a point guard, but Brown thought that the playmaker role was too much of a burden for any rookie to handle and thought that the point guard is the hardest position to play in the NBA at that time. And for Simmons, who was never pegged as a point guard his entire life, it might be a difficult transition for him.[xii]

This was evident during the Summer League games as he made some timely errors especially when he was dribbling the ball in traffic. At 6'10", it was difficult for him to handle the ball against several small players because of how much easier it was for the ball to be stripped. As such, Simmons lost the ball several times to smaller guards when he was trying to dribble the ball against tough defenses.

However, Ben Simmons did not close his mind to the idea of playing point guard and even said that he was willing to make the transition if ever his coach wanted him to do so. He definitely was trying to be a point guard during Summer League and some analysts and experts thought he was becoming too unselfish. However, such things are part of the growing pains of a budding star just trying to find his place in the NBA.

When Summer League ended, Ben Simmons was named to the First Team after finishing with averages of 10.8 points, 7.7 rebounds, and 5.5 assists. He struggled to put points up on the board and was still adjusting to the physicality and defensive sets of NBA-level basketball. He also was clearly trying to set his teammates up more instead of asserting himself as a scorer, and defenses were also keen on letting Simmons' teammates beat them instead of giving open scoring opportunities to the incoming NBA rookie. And oftentimes, his teammates failed to deliver.

But that could all change come the start of the NBA season when Simmons had a chance to play together with better teammates and developing young talents such as Joel Embiid and Jahlil Okafor. This time, he would not be the center of their opponents' defensive attention as Ben Simmons would have teammates that were able to finish baskets when he found them open. Things were only going to get brighter for Ben Simmons, or so everyone thought.

During the final scrimmage of the Philadelphia 76ers' training camp, Ben Simmons sprained his right ankle. After further evaluation and tests, it was revealed that he fractured a bone in his right foot. The injury kept him off the roster when the season began, but it was estimated that he would be back in three to four months of healing and rehabilitation following surgery.

After surgery and during rehabilitation, Ben Simmons worked hard. He put in a lot of effort in the weight room to make sure he put on some much-needed muscle mass that would allow him to finish better through contact against bigger and stronger NBA defenders. Pegged at 230 pounds during draft night, he jacked up to 250 pounds. He even said that he only weight about 217 during his LSU days and had bulked up and gained over 30 pounds of muscle mass since then.[xiii]

Putting on a lot of muscle weight would only help Ben Simmons take the grind of playing in the NBA since his style of play requires him to be strong and heavy enough to power his way to the basket for scoring opportunities. And judging from how he struggled with his scoring during the Summer League, Simmons needed to become stronger so that he could continue to play the freight train style of basketball he was known for in high school and college.

However, Ben Simmons' NBA debut would have to wait until the 2017-18 season. In February 2017, the Philadelphia 76ers announced that he was going to miss the entire 2016-17 season after further testing and evaluation showed that his ankle did not heal the way they wanted it to. Simmons was heartbroken because all he wanted to do was suit up for his team to help them win games.[xiv] But that would have to wait because at that point everyone needed him to be fully healthy. Playing in the NBA is a very physically taxing endeavor.

Failing to suit up in what was supposed to be his rookie season did not dampen Ben Simmons' spirits, however. He was still determined to get back on the court and showcase how truly one-of-a-kind he is as a basketball talent and budding generational star in the NBA. And the league was not ready for the storm that Ben Simmons was cooking up while he was biding his time to make his NBA debut.

The Long-Awaited Debut Season, Becoming Rookie of the Year

Throughout Ben Simmons' absence during the 2016-17 season, the Philadelphia 76ers continued to struggle to contend for the playoffs. Though they had improved admirably, the Sixers were still one of the worst teams in the NBA and were set on getting another high lottery draft pick in the upcoming draft. However, they did have a few bright spots that season.

The one thing that got Sixers fans feeling optimistic during the 2016-17 season was Joel Embiid, who finally made a season debut after missing his first two seasons due to injuries. The former Kansas standout and one-time Montverde Academy player was Philadelphia's best player that season. However, he only played 31 games as the Sixers were slowly easing him in to avoid injury. Despite that, he still managed to show the full package of his talents and made everyone understand why the Philadelphia 76ers were so patient with his recovery.

And after only winning 28 games, which was an 18-game improvement from the previous year, the Sixers were in a good spot to land a top lottery pick. They ended up getting the third overall pick but traded it to the Boston Celtics for their first overall pick. That means that the Philadelphia 76ers were in the best spot to draft Markelle Fultz, who was regarded as the best player of the 2017 NBA Draft.

Drafting a ball-handling and scoring point guard with their first overall pick meant that the Sixers would have to place the returning Ben Simmons at the forward position even though Brett Brown had previously announced that he wanted to play Simmons more at the point months before the Philadelphia 76ers drafted Markelle Fultz. Though nobody thought that this would become a major problem for the Sixers, it could still spell minor issues for a team that was still looking to make their mark after years of suffering at the bottom of the standings.

However, the reason why the Sixers were envisioning both Simmons and Fultz together on the floor at the same time was not for both of the incoming rookies to share ball-handling duties. Rather, it was more of a way to make things easier for Simmons on the defensive end as Brett Brown thought that he would struggle to defend smaller and quicker point guards if he ever played that position. They needed a shorter and quicker man to take the defensive load off of Simmons' shoulders. And in the one season he spent in college, Fultz showed how capable he is at the defensive end.[xv]

Brett Brown also added that he was still planning on making Ben Simmons the team's full-time point guard on the offensive end in the sense that he would be responsible for a lot of the ball-handling and playmaking duties, which are essentially the jobs of a point guard. However, he also thought that Fultz was still going to play to his strengths as a ball-dominant point guard from time to time.[xv]

After all, in this pace-and-space era where the best teams in the NBA do not necessarily rely on one player to handle the ball and make plays but more on ball and people movement, it is essential for a franchise to have two or more players that are willing to find open teammates. The Cleveland Cavaliers ended up winning a championship in 2016 while relying on LeBron James and Kyrie Irving juggling ball-handling duties. Steph Curry, Draymond Green, and Kevin Durant of the Golden State Warriors also found success as a trio of unselfish stars willing enough to become playmakers from time to time.

On the part of Simmons and Fultz, many thought that it was all going to be part of the process for them to learn how to play together in the backcourt while sharing ball-handling duties. It did not hurt that the Sixers' other star, Joel Embiid, also knew how to play both on and off the ball and could also make timely plays for others when he saw an opening.

Unfortunately for the Sixers, they saw another top draft pick suffering an injury even before the season started. Markelle Fultz had a shoulder injury that altered the way he shot the ball. He did still suit up for the Sixers that season, but it was evident that he was not himself especially when he was shooting the ball from the perimeter. The injury was more of a nerve disorder, which also caused Fultz to lose confidence in his ability to shoot the ball.[xvi] As such, he hardly played at all during his rookie season. That meant that Ben Simmons would have to play the point guard position on a full-time basis.

However, even after fully recovering from his injury, Ben Simmons could not avoid early criticism and speculations. There were doubts regarding his strength and conditioning as well as his ability to score after resting the majority of the time during his one-year recovery process.[xvii] One can easily understand the doubts because Ben Simmons still has not proven himself in the NBA and mostly stayed away from any basketball-related activities during his recuperation.

Ever the confident young man, Ben Simmons thought that he improved every aspect of his game in time for his much-awaited NBA debut. He said that he still thought that there was hardly anyone that could guard him one-on-one off the dribble especially when he brought the ball up the length of the court. Simmons even said that he also expects himself to be a great leader for the Philadelphia 76ers. And he was not expecting to be one of the top rookies that season because he was not aiming to be one. Instead, he was already aiming at the guys at the top of the food chain in the NBA instead of competing against his fellow incoming rookies.[xvii]

Ben Simmons might have been away from basketball when he was recovering from injury, but it was how he prepared himself physically that made him confident that he was going to make an impact on the NBA. He spent a lot of time in the weight room working on his strength and conditioning. He also mentally prepared himself for the grind of a full NBA season. And it was evident how much he had improved when he was dominating five-on-five scrimmages and was also often seen dunking hard even during practices. As

Markelle Fultz said, he felt sorry for any team that was going to have to go up against Ben Simmons.[xvii]

Of course, Ben Simmons did not disappoint his believers when the season started. In his season debut on October 18, 2017, the big point guard showcased his wares in a matchup against John Wall and the Washington Wizards. In that five-point loss for the Sixers, he put up 18 points, ten rebounds, five assists, and two steals in only his first official regular season game in the NBA. Then, just three days later, he nearly put up a triple-double after finishing a loss to the Toronto Raptors with 18 points, ten rebounds, and eight assists. Simmons was the first player since Oscar Robertson in the 1960s to put up at least ten points, ten rebounds, and five assists in his first three games.

It did not take long for Ben Simmons to put up his first career triple-double. On October 23, Ben Simmons finished a win over the Detroit Pistons with 21 points, 12 rebounds, and ten assists. He officially became the only player since two others did it in the 1960s (Oscar Robertson and Art Williams) to put up a triple-double in his first four regular-season games in the NBA. Since then, the wins kept piling up for the Sixers after losing their first three games.

In a win over the Dallas Mavericks on October 28, Ben Simmons had a new career high in points after shooting 10 out of 15 from the floor and scoring 23 points to go along with seven rebounds, eight assists, and three steals. Two days later, he broke that mark by going for 24 points, seven rebounds, and nine assists in a win over the Houston Rockets.

On November 3, Ben Simmons recorded his second career triple-double in a win over the Indiana Pacers. In that game, he had 14 points, 11 rebounds, and a new career high of 11 assists. Later that month in a loss to the Golden State Warriors on November 18, Simmons dished out 12 dimes to record a new career high in assists. He also finished that game with 23 points.

Simmons once again broke his career mark in scoring after a fantastic win over the Utah Jazz on November 20. In that game, he made 13 of his 24 shots to finish the game with 27 points together with ten rebounds and four steals. But it did not take long for him to break that mark as he went on to have the best game of his young career in a win over the Washington Wizards on November 29. Ben Simmons had career highs in points and rebounds in that performance after he finished with 31 points and 18 rebounds.

In a narrow loss to the Los Angeles Lakers on December 7, Ben Simmons looked a lot like Magic Johnson after finishing the game with his third career triple-double. He had 12 points, 12 rebounds, and a new career high of 15 assists. Then, in four of his next five games, Simmons looked like a legitimate star point guard after tallying double-digit assists.

As defenses adjusted to his style of play, Ben Simmons began to slow down a bit during the latter part of December up to the first weeks of 2018. However, he broke his slump on January 24, 2018, after going for his first triple-double of the new calendar year. In that win over the Chicago Bulls, Simmons had finished with 19 points, 17 rebounds, and 14 assists. After that performance, Ben Simmons went on a 27-game streak of scoring ten or more points as he continued to stay consistent as a scorer for the vastly-improved Philadelphia 76ers.

But even though Ben Simmons was putting up some of the best numbers an NBA rookie could average and the best all-around statistics for any player not named LeBron James or Russell Westbrook, he was not named as an All-Star starter or reserve. However, Ben Simmons had more fan votes than All-Star guards Victor Oladipo, Bradley Beal, and John Wall and was third overall behind Kyrie Irving and DeMar DeRozan in the Eastern Conference guards.

However, coaches and the media clearly were not sold on the sensational rookie from Australia as they gave their votes to the veteran guards in the East. Before the All-Star festivities started, Simmons was averaging 16.4 points, 7.8 rebounds, 7.3 assists, and 1.9 steals. Those are clearly numbers worthy of an All-Star guard, but he still managed to get snubbed.

However, Ben Simmons excelled in the Rising Stars Challenge during the All-Star Weekend. He helped lead Team World to a blowout victory over Team USA with a spectacular performance of 11 points, six rebounds, 13 assists, and four steals. However, he would not get named MVP of the event. It was shooter Bogdan Bogdanovic who got the MVP over Simmons.

After the All-Star festivities, Simmons went on to show that he should have been an All-Star. In his first game since the break, he had 32 points, seven rebounds, and 11 assists in a win over the Chicago Bulls. Then, on March 4, he tied his career high in assists after going for 12 points and 15 assists in a loss to the Milwaukee Bucks. Two days after that, he led a win over the Charlotte Hornets with 16 points, eight rebounds, and 13 assists.

On March 13, Ben Simmons recorded his seven triple-double after finishing a win over the Indiana Pacers with ten points, 13 rebounds, and ten assists. And after going for 13 points, ten rebounds, and 13 assists in a win over the New York Knicks, he became only the third rookie in the history of the NBA to reach 1,000 points, 500 rebounds, and 500 assists. Oscar Robertson and Magic Johnson were the only other rookies to achieve such a feat.

Ben Simmons would again make history on March 19. In that win over the Charlotte Hornets, he became only the third rookie in NBA history to finish a game with a triple-double without incurring even one turnover. He had 11 points, 12 rebounds, and 15 assists. He followed that up five days later with his 10th triple-double of the season when he had 15 points, 12 rebounds, and 13 assists against the Minnesota Timberwolves in a win.

A game after that, Ben Simmons narrowly missed another triple-double when he had seven points, 13 rebounds, and 11 assists. However, with that performance, he topped Allen Iverson's team record in assists for a rookie. He tied his career high in assists on April 1 with 15 dimes to go along with 20 points and eight rebounds. In the last six games he played up to that point, he averaged 12.3 points, 10.7 rebounds, and 11.7 assists. More importantly, the Philadelphia 76ers were in the middle of a terrific winning streak that was seemingly just a dream a season ago.

On April 6, Ben Simmons finished a win over the Cleveland Cavaliers with 27 points, 15 rebounds, and 13 assists for his 12th triple-double. That was arguably his best game of the regular season and he went head-to-head with LeBron James who had 44 points and a triple-double. Philadelphia won 13 consecutive games with that win over the Cavs. They would then win three more games to finish the season with 16 consecutive wins, which was a franchise record.

Finishing the season with a record of 52 wins as against losses, the Philadelphia 76ers had their most wins since Allen Iverson led the team back in 2001. And just two years before, they only won ten games. That goes to show that Ben Simmons was indeed a game-changer of a player as he went on to help turn the Sixers into playoff contenders seemingly overnight.

In 81 regular season games for Ben Simmons, the rookie averaged 15.8 points, 8.1 rebounds, 8.2 assists, and 1.7 steals. He shot 54.5% from the field and was one of the most efficient scorers in the league. On top of that, he was one of the few players that averaged at least 15 points, eight rebounds, and eight assists that season. He had a total of 12 triple-doubles. In that regard, he had the second most triple-doubles for a rookie. Only Oscar Robertson, who had 26 triple-doubles, had more as a rookie.

More importantly, Ben Simmons and the Philadelphia 76ers were on their way to their first playoff appearance since 2012. They had the third seed in the East and seemingly fast-tracked the process they had been working on for more than a handful of seasons already. As such, it was clear that both Ben Simmons and center Joel Embiid were worth the wait.

Ben Simmons would make his playoff debut on April 14, against the Miami Heat. He narrowly missed what would have been his first career triple-double in the playoffs after going for 17 points, nine rebounds, and 14 assists in that blowout win in Game 1. The Heat would win Game 2, but the Philadelphia 76ers never looked back after that loss.

In Game 3, Ben Simmons finished with 19 points, 12 rebounds, seven assists, and four steals in a 20-point win. Two days later in Game 4, he had 17 points, 13 rebounds, ten assists, and four steals for his first playoff triple-double. He became the first rookie since 1980 to record a triple-double in the playoffs. The last one to do it was Magic Johnson. He also became only the fifth player after Kareem Abdul-Jabbar, Magic Johnson, Jerry Lucas, and Tom Gola to achieve such a feat.

Ben Simmons and the Sixers wrapped the series up in five games after beating the Miami Heat on April 24. He finished Game 5 with 14 points, ten rebounds, six assists, and two steals. Ben Simmons averaged crazy numbers of 18.2 points, 10.6 rebounds, nine assists, and 2.4 steals in the Philadelphia 76ers' first-round win over the Miami Heat.

The second round was going to be much more difficult. The Sixers were set to match up with the top-seeded Boston Celtics, who were known for their suffocating style of defense. In that regard, they limited the

Philadelphia 76ers' best players in Game 1. In that loss, Simmons had 18 points but performed subpar in all other areas.

Game 2 was the worst that Ben had played in recent memory. Simmons failed to score a field goal in four tries and his only point came from a lone free throw. The key was that the Celtics were shrinking the floor and daring Ben Simmons to shoot and try to beat them from the perimeter instead of allowing him to force his way inside the paint. The Sixers ended up losing that game.

That poor performance exposed Ben Simmons and his most glaring weakness—shooting. He became the subject of ridicule because he could not hit a perimeter shot to help his team in tough situations. And even if he tried to get to the basket, the one thing that the Boston Celtics were willing to do was become physical with him. They could contain his drives but still managed to put a lot of defenders on him even if he slashed his way to the basket. On top of that, the Celtics were putting different people on him to give him different looks.

However, Ben Simmons thought that his poor performance in Game 2 was more self-inflicted. He believed that he was to blame for that performance instead of the Boston Celtics' defense.[xviii] He said that he was thinking too much instead of simplifying the game in his mind. As such, he ended up struggling with the looks he was given and the Sixers were headed into Game 3 down 0-2.

In Game 3, the Philadelphia 76ers fought hard on their own home floor but still could not beat the Boston Celtics. Simmons had 16 points, eight rebounds, and eight assists in that three-point loss. Down 0-3, the Sixers did not have history on their side as they were headed to Game 4. Luckily, they avoided the sweep after winning Game 4. In that lone series win, Simmons had 18 points, 13 rebounds, and five assists.

The Celtics completed the series win in Game 5. In that elimination game, Simmons had 18 points, eight rebounds, and six assists.

Even though Ben Simmons and the Philadelphia 76ers ended their season with a loss in the second round, there was a lot of optimism on their side. For one, both Ben Simmons and Joel Embiid were headed into stardom as the team's newest star one-two punch. Second, they had broken a long playoff drought and seemingly completed the process of rebuilding. And third, Ben Simmons was only going to be a better player after his rookie year.

Ben Simmons was also in the running for the Rookie of the Year award, which was to be announced after the conclusion of the season. However, the winner of the award was a tough one to decide because there were a lot of outstanding rookies that season. Among the many newcomers that stood out, the three finalists for the award were Ben Simmons, Donovan Mitchell, and Jayson Tatum.

Though Jayson Tatum did not have the strongest case for the Rookie of the Year award, he still managed to prove that he was just as good and capable as the two others who were vying for that accolade. He averaged 13.9 points and five rebounds for the East-leading Boston Celtics that season. And though his numbers did not amaze anyone, what people had to look at was that the Celtics were a very deep team that relied on several wing players.

The Boston Celtics had seven players averaging double-digit numbers concerning scoring and were relying more on a team-oriented style of offense after high-scoring guard Kyrie Irving went down with an injury. In that sense, the best case that Tatum could make was that he was a consistent contributor for a team that had a chance at the NBA title that season. In a way, Jayson Tatum was the best rookie concerning team accomplishments.

Meanwhile, the only other player that had a very good case for the Rookie of the Year award was the Utah Jazz's Donovan Mitchell. Drafted 13th overall in the 2017 NBA Draft, the 6'3" shooting guard did not get as much attention as the other rookies in his class even after performing admirably in his two seasons with Louisville in college. However, he surprised everyone with his explosive athleticism, high-scoring prowess, and ability to play off the pick-and-roll as a ball-dominant shooting guard. Donovan Mitchell averaged 20.5 points, 3.7 rebounds, 3.7 assists, and 1.5 steals as a rookie. He led all rookies in scoring.

Though he did not start his rookie season very well, it was only after the Jazz realized how good of a player Mitchell is that they started giving him more looks and possessions. They ran the offense through their rookie guard and still managed to win 50 games that season after losing star player Gordon Hayward to free agency during the 2017 offseason. In a way, Mitchell's scoring and ability to manufacture offense for himself and his teammates made up for Hayward's loss.

Finally, there was Ben Simmons. There was nothing else to say about Simmons that has not already been said. The way he played the point guard position for the Sixers, who improved so much with his addition, spoke for itself. He was the electrifying and calming presence that Philadelphia needed to fast-track their rebuilding process. And in helping his team do so, Simmons nearly averaged a triple-double as a rookie and was regularly putting up the best all-around numbers of any first-year player since Magic Johnson back in 1980. Moreover, he had a bigger role for the Sixers than Tatum did for the Celtics and also finished with more wins that Donovan Mitchell.

As great of a rookie as Ben Simmons was that season, the biggest argument against Ben Simmons' candidacy as the 2018 Rookie of the Year was that he was not a true rookie in the strict sense of that word. He was drafted back in 2016, played Summer League games, and trained with his team. In that case, many would argue that he already had the advantage over all of the rookies that were drafted in 2017 because he had already spent a full year as an NBA player training with NBA-level staff and coaches.

However, the rules were clear that an NBA rookie is someone who has not played a regular season game in the league. As such, because Ben Simmons failed to suit up for a game in the year he was drafted, he was still a rookie. And such an instance, after all, was not unique to Simmons' case. David Robinson, who was drafted in 1987 but had to serve the military for two years, was the Rookie of the Year in 1990. Blake Griffin, who was drafted 2009 but missed a year due to injury, was named the 2011 Rookie of the Year.

But some would say that Robinson's and Griffin's cases were different in the sense that they really were dominating their respective rookie seasons to the point that there was no other rookie that performed as well as they did. In fact, both players ended up winning their Rookie of the Year awards unanimously and were clearly head and shoulders above the competition. But that was not the case for Ben Simmons as he was not the only outstanding newcomer in the NBA during the 2017-18 season.

When the NBA awards night came shortly after the Golden State Warriors won their second consecutive championship, the Rookie of the Year accolade went to Ben Simmons. The Australian may not have been named to the All-Star team and did indeed have his doubters as a rookie, but he still won 90 of the possible 101 first-place votes for the Rookie of the Year award. It appeared that Donovan Mitchell, who only got 11 first-place votes, was a far second to Simmons for the award.

With Ben Simmons winning Rookie of the Year and NBA All-Rookie First Team honors, the sky was the limit for the 21-year-old Australian sensation as he still had several more years under his belt to improve on his weaknesses. He had already proven himself as a force to be reckoned with in the NBA and was only going to get better as he progressed through what was still the early parts of his professional basketball career.

First All-Star Appearance

After wrapping up a successful rookie season for himself and the Philadelphia 76ers, Ben Simmons knew that the rest of the NBA had already scouted him and were only going to give him tougher looks on the offensive end. In that regard, the only thing he could do to make sure he could continue to contribute to the success of his team was improve his game.

One of the first things he worked on during the 2018 offseason was his jump shot. Coming into his second year in the NBA, Ben Simmons' most glaring weakness was indeed his outside shooting. This was not a secret. Not only was he struggling to make his jumpers, but he also was not willing to even attempt outside shots as seen from his shooting numbers.

In Ben Simmons' rookie season, 78.7% of his shot attempts were close shots that were within ten feet of the basket. Not to anyone's surprise, most of those shots were near the rim as 46.2% of his attempts were at most three feet away from the goal. Meanwhile, he was even hesitant to take close midrange jumpers as only 17.4% of his attempts came from somewhere between 10 to 16 feet away from the basket. It was rare for anyone to see him taking long jumpers that were beyond 16 feet. He only took 11 shots from beyond the three-point line and made none of them. His free throw shooting also was just as bad after shooting only 56% from the line.

For someone who has been playing basketball all his life, Ben Simmons was a rare case for a guard of his caliber and skillset. There are a lot of players in the NBA that are not particularly the best jump shooters, but they are not afraid of taking those shots. Meanwhile, Simmons did not even look like he was interested in taking a jump shot in his rookie season.

There are those that would say that Simmons' IQ was high enough for him to know that it would be unwise for a struggling jump shooter such as himself to take long shots. Simmons also knew that he was better off taking his man to the basket where he was simply unstoppable after shooting 74.4% from within three feet away from the rim.

But the one thing that was clear was that Simmons' inability and unwillingness to shoot jumpers did not do his team any good. The Boston Celtics proved that when they simply left the Australian point guard out on the perimeter and clogged the lane to take away driving opportunities while also shrinking the floor to allow less spacing for the rest of the players on the floor for the Sixers. Such a defensive tactic clearly hurt the Sixers as they fell to the Celtics in five games.

Everyone knew that Ben Simmons was not going to be Klay Thompson in an instant or even a respectable jump shooter after just a few months. But he knew for a fact that being a willing shooter already adds value to his team because that will make defenses respect him a bit more out of fear that he might make one shot from the perimeter if left too wide open.[xix]

In that regard, Ben Simmons spent his summer training his jump shot with his half-brother Liam Tribe-Simmons, a former assistant for UC Riverside. While he was not going to transform into JJ Redick with just a few months of training under his belt and was not even expected to become a consistent shooter his entire career, it was still important to make defenses fear the possibility that he might make shots from the perimeter or even from the three-point line. That means that he would open up more driving and passing opportunities for himself or at least improve his team's spacing.

Also, Ben Simmons spent the summer training his physique in Los Angeles and knew for a fact that his greatest asset would always be his ability to get to the basket and score efficiently near the rim. He resumed lifting weights while undergoing different strength and conditioning workouts to improve his overall physique and ability to take contact. And coming into his second year in the NBA, Simmons was arguably in the best shape of his life and looked more jacked and ripped than he ever was in his career.[xx] That would only spell doom for defenders willing to try to get in Simmons' way when he is making his way to the basket like a freight train.

When the season started, Ben Simmons put in a good effort in the Sixers' season debut game against the Boston Celtics. In that game on October 16, 2018, he had 19 points, 15 rebounds, eight assists, four steals, and two blocks. However, the Philadelphia 76ers ended up losing that game to the Celtics. But two days later in a win over the Chicago Bulls, he had his first triple-double of the season after going for 13 points, 13 rebounds, and 11 assists.

Ben Simmons, who played forward a lot of times during the early parts of the season to make room for the adjusting Markelle Fultz, had another triple-double in a loss to the Milwaukee Bucks on October 24. He finished that game with 14 points, 13 rebounds, and 11 assists and was evidently still responsible for the majority of the team's ball-handling duties.

Though Ben Simmons flirted with triple-doubles a lot of times in the Sixers' first few games, the team did not have the hottest starts and the second-year Australian also struggled a bit from the field. The biggest issue was arguably because the Sixers were trying to play him and the struggling Fultz together at the same time, which caused spacing issues.

However, because Markelle Fultz clearly was not yet physically and mentally ready to make a difference, the Sixers decided to shut him down. His shoulder was still bothering him and he would not play another game the entire season. The Philadelphia 76ers also added a third star to complement their budding twosome of Simmons and Embiid. They sent Dario Saric and Robert Covington to the Minnesota Timberwolves in exchange for disgruntled All-Star wing Jimmy Butler. As such, there was another player that could handle the scoring and ball-handling load from the backcourt position other than Ben Simmons.

The midseason changes allowed Ben Simmons more room to operate both as a scorer and as a playmaker. He had his third triple-double of the season on December 16 after finishing a win over the Cleveland Cavaliers with 22 points, 11 rebounds, and 14 assists. Three days later, he went for 13 points, 12 rebounds, and ten assists in a win over the New York Knicks. Then, on December 27, he tallied yet another triple-double after going for 13 points, 14 rebounds, and 12 assists in a win over Utah.

Fresh off the New Year, Ben Simmons had his season-high in points on January 2, 2019, in a win over the Phoenix Suns. He had 29 points that game. Three days after that, he went for his first triple-double of 2019 when he led a win over the Dallas Mavericks with 20 points, 13 rebounds, and 11 assists.

On January 11, Ben Simmons had another great triple-double performance when he went for 23 points, ten rebounds, and 15 assists against the Atlanta Hawks in a loss. He had an even better game just two days later when he led a win over the New York Knicks. Ben Simmons finished the game with 20 points, nine assists, and a new career high of 22 rebounds.

After going for 20 points, 11 rebounds, and nine assists in a win over the Timberwolves on January 15, Simmons became the second-fastest player to reach 2,000 points, 1,000 rebounds, and 1,000 assists. He did so in 125 games and passed Magic Johnson's record of 131 games. Only Oscar Robertson has done it in fewer games. Even LeBron James needed 158 games to reach that milestone.

But Ben Simmons was not yet done piling up ridiculous all-around numbers. In a win over the San Antonio Spurs on January 23, he had 21 points, ten rebounds, and 15 assists. A little over a week after that, he was named a reserve for the Eastern Conference All-Stars. Though his numbers were similar to that of his rookie year, it was how he had already made his name as one of the premier players in the NBA that got him the nod from the voters this time.

Ben Simmons also participated in the Rising Stars Game as a member of Team World. Though his team failed to get the win this time, he was Team World's most outstanding player after going for 28 points, five rebounds, six assists, and three steals. As a member of Team LeBron during the All-Star Game, Ben

Simmons helped his squad win by going for ten points, six rebounds, and seven assists.

Shortly after the All-Star break, Ben Simmons had back-to-back triple-doubles for the first time that season. He first went for 11 points, 13 rebounds, and 11 assists on February 28 in a win over the Oklahoma City Thunder. The second one came when he went for 25 points, 15 rebounds, and 11 assists in a narrow loss to the Golden State Warriors two days later.

After recording ninth and 10th triple-doubles that season, Ben Simmons went on to average 16.6 points, 7.6 rebounds, and 7.2 assists in his final 17 games during the regular season because there was no need for him to produce more. This was due to the midseason acquisition of floor-spacing forward Tobias Harris, who was putting up 20 points on a regular basis for the Los Angeles Clippers before getting traded to the Sixers. With Simmons, Embiid, Butler, and Harris in the fold, Philadelphia now has its own version of a super team in the Eastern Conference.

The regular season ended with Philadelphia winning 51 games as against 31 losses. They were once again the third seed in the East headed into the playoffs. Meanwhile, the first Australian NBA All-Star went on to average 16.9 points, 8.8 rebounds, and 7.7 assists during the regular season. Ben Simmons also shot an improved 56.3% from the field and was one of the most efficient scorers in the entire NBA that season.

In the first round of the playoffs, the Brooklyn Nets managed to pull off an upset over the Sixers in a surprisingly poor outing for Simmons. In that loss, Ben Simmons only had nine points, seven rebounds, and three assists. Nevertheless, he more than made up for that poor performance by going for his second playoff triple-double in Game 2. In that win, he had 18 points, ten rebounds, and 12 assists.

Then, before Game 3, Brooklyn Nets forward Jared Dudley said that Ben Simmons is only an average player when he is kept in the half-court and is not given the chance to play in transition. Though Ben Simmons dismissed this comment,[xxi] he proved that he was anything but an average player with his performance in Game 3. In that win, he went for 31 points, nine assists, two steals, and three blocks. The Sixers would then win the next two games as Ben Simmons and his team bounced back from that Game 1 upset.

Chapter 5: International Career

Ben Simmons has been playing for the Australian Men's National Basketball Team since he was 15 years old. The first time he suited up for the Australian Boomers, which is what their national team is called, was during the FIBA Under-17 World Championships back in 2012. For such a young man, Simmons played well in that tournament and managed to lead Australia to a second-place finish when they lost to the United States in the finals. He averaged nine points and 5.4 rebounds in that tournament.

The next time Ben Simmons suited up for Australia was in 2013 back when he was still a high school standout in Montverde. He was the youngest player on that team and was only one of two teenagers (18-year-old Dante Exum was the other one) playing for Australia. Although he did not get a lot of minutes in the FIBA Oceania Championships for Men, Australia still won the gold medal. Simmons averaged just two points.

Ben Simmons had several more opportunities to try to represent Australia in international competitions. In 2014, he said that he wanted to play for his country, but the high schooler was cut from the final roster. In 2016, he also wanted to play for Australia in the Olympics, but he opted not to because he was preparing for what should have been his first season in the NBA. However, as early as 2017, Ben Simmons had already manifested his intentions of wanting to play for the Boomers in the 2020 Tokyo Olympics.

Chapter 6: Personal Life

Ben Simmons is a dual citizen of both the United States and Australia. His father David Simmons is an American, a former professional basketball player in Australia, and a naturalized citizen of that country. His mother Julie Simmons is a native of Australia. Because Julie was previously married before meeting David, Ben Simmons has four half-siblings other than his sister Olivia. He is the youngest of six children in the Simmons household.

Most of Ben Simmons' family members are and have been involved in sports. His father was a former professional basketball player and assistant coach. His half-brother Liam Tribe-Simmons was a former assistant at UC Riverside and later became Ben's shooting coach. Emily Tribe was a member of the rowing team in Washington State and is married to NFL player Michael Bush. His sister Olivia Simmons played basketball at Arizona State. And finally, Sean Tribe works as a sports agent.

Ben Simmons has been romantically linked to American celebrities. The most prominent celebrity he has dated is Kendall Jenner of the famous Kardashian-Jenner family. They started dating when Simmons was still fresh off of his rookie season in the NBA. Ben spent most of the summer of 2018 in Los Angeles where Kendall's family is based.

Chapter 7: Impact on Basketball

It might be too early in his career to say that Ben Simmons has had a significant impact on basketball, but he has already made his mark on the sport just because of how innovative and novel his style of play is. Never in the history of the NBA has anyone seen a legitimate 6'10" point guard playing the position at a level higher than most of the other natural playmakers in the league.

Even though Ben Simmons has the height and length of a power forward and athletic abilities of a small forward, the skills he has are more or less reminiscent of a point guard. He can bring the ball up the length of the court with ease because of his quickness and ball-handling skills. His ability to drive and break defenses down allows him to create wide-open looks for teammates. And when he sees an opening, he is a willing passer that can see over the top of most defenders and make passes that not even the best point guards in the world can see.

And when Ben Simmons is scoring the ball, he has the finishing abilities of a forward because of his incredible physical gifts but he can create such looks for himself because he is quicker, more explosive, and a lot more skillful than most forwards in the NBA. That means that he is a matchup nightmare because he can simply blow by big but slow defenders and power through smaller guards.

With these physical attributes and skills, Ben Simmons fits the mold of today's positionless basketball because he can seemingly play any position he wants due to his size and to his all-around skills. You can practically put him offensively and defensively in four positions but can still get the same production out of Ben Simmons.

Speaking of positionless basketball, Ben Simmons' impact can be seen and measured in the way he has fit the current era he plays in. Some people may say that he is the second coming of Magic Johnson or that his LeBron 2.0, but he is a different player compared to those two. He is a unicorn or a player that is 6'10" or taller but has the skills of a guard and mobility of a wing. That makes him the perfect point guard that any team can have in this pace-and-space era that relies on players that are unselfish and skilled on the offensive end and can also cover any position on the defensive part of the game.

That said, Ben Simmons can be regarded as the new breed of NBA point guards because of how he is changing the way the game is played. Together with some of the other unicorns in the NBA today, his impact can be seen in how he makes the game look so easy for a man of his size. In that regard, he is proving that size is not the factor that defines an NBA player's position. He is instead showing to the world that skill is what is most important in determining how someone should play in the NBA.

As Ben Simmons continues to define traditional NBA positions, we might very well see younger kids patterning their games after the all-around abilities of this 6'10" giant point guard from Australia. And several years from now, it might not even be a surprise if we see players 6'6" or taller playing point guard at All-Star levels as well.

Chapter 8: Legacy and Future

Ben Simmons is still in the early stages of his career and has not yet carved a legacy that he can call his own. Nevertheless, he is getting there and is no doubt one of the few players in the NBA that can make a lasting legacy in the coming years. That said, Simmons is also a player that continues to carry the legacies of former NBA stars.

As a big point guard, one would say that Ben Simmons has continued a legacy that started with Oscar Robertson, who was then succeeded by Magic Johnson in the '80s. We then saw the likes of Penny Hardaway and Jason Kidd as the big point guards of the '90s. And although we do not regard him as a point guard, LeBron James is every bit of a big playmaker that Oscar, Magic, and Penny were. And now, when James is seemingly in the deeper stages of his career, we are seeing the emergence of a legitimate big point guard in Ben Simmons.

To say that Ben Simmons is a big point guard is an understatement. At 6'10" and with a muscular frame that is reminiscent of a Greek god statue, Simmons is a gigantic playmaker that makes us remember the good old days when Magic Johnson was running the Los Angeles Lakers offense at a height of 6'9". Simmons is bigger and much more athletic than Magic but has the same skills that made Johnson a Hall of Fame legend.

As such, the Australian playmaker has the potential to one day become just as great of a legend as Robertson and Johnson are given that he is not only bigger than those players but is still very young. But as of now, he is carrying a legacy that started with those players and will continue to carry it at a level that would not disappoint his predecessors.

As a Sixer, Ben Simmons continues a legacy of Philadelphia All-Stars that seemingly halted when Allen Iverson left the team in the middle of the 2000s. While the 76ers produced some All-Star players since then, none of them have the caliber and potential for greatness that Ben Simmons and even teammate Joel Embiid have. Together, these two franchise cornerstones are tasked with the responsibility of bringing back the glory days of the Philadelphia 76ers.

In the early years that the two have played together, they have already shown that they are capable of carrying the team the same way former stars such as Allen Iverson, Charles Barkley, Moses Malone, Julius Erving, and Wilt Chamberlain did. And if Ben Simmons keeps improving and striving for greatness, he and Joel Embiid will undoubtedly be in the running for a title in the future so long as the pieces and circumstances are right.

Finally, Ben Simmons has become the standard bearer of Australian basketball in the NBA. There have not been a lot of Australians in the NBA. We saw Luc Longley winning titles in the '90s with the Chicago Bulls but not quite playing to the level of a star. Then

Andrew Bogut was selected first overall in 2005, became a double-double threat, and won a title with the Golden State Warriors. Then there are players such as Dante Exum and Joe Ingles, who have both been good role players in the league today.

Nevertheless, as productive as Australians have been in the NBA, there was never truly an All-Star from that continent before Ben Simmons. He is the first Australian player to be named an NBA All-Star and is now quickly rising as perhaps the greatest basketball product the country has ever produced. Though it is too early to say that he already has a better career than any of the other Australians that have played in the NBA, it certainly is not wrong to say that the talent and potential that he has make him the face of Australian basketball. As such, we might even see more Australians coming to the NBA in the future, not only as productive role players but as stars as well.

Regarding Ben Simmons' future, one cannot say for sure what the next years will be like for a player of his talent and attributes. He might follow a path similar to Magic Johnson or LeBron James, or he might carve his own destiny and legacy in the league. We certainly will see him earning more All-Star selections, but it is too tough of a call to say that he might hoist a championship later in his career.

However, what is as certain as day is that Ben Simmons will continue to change the way basketball is played just by being himself. He continues to define logic, expectations, and even traditions as he has helped mold the point guard position into something new and novel. Some might say he is not a point guard in the strict sense of the word and others may say that he does not have a definite position in the NBA because of his uncanny combination of talent and size. But there is a position that Ben Simmons has been playing at a high level ever since he learned how to play basketball. And that is the position of a star.

Final Word/About the Author

I was born and raised in Norwalk, Connecticut. Growing up, I could often be found spending many nights watching basketball, soccer, and football matches with my father in the family living room. I love sports and everything that sports can embody. I believe that sports are one of most genuine forms of competition, heart, and determination. I write my works to learn more about influential athletes in the hopes that from my writing, you the reader can walk away inspired to put in an equal if not greater amount of hard work and perseverance to pursue your goals. If you enjoyed *Ben Simmons: The Inspiring Story of One of Basketball's Rising All-Stars,* please leave a review! Also, you can read more of my works on *Roger Federer, Novak Djokovic, Andrew Luck, Rob Gronkowski, Brett Favre, Calvin Johnson, Drew Brees, J.J. Watt, Colin Kaepernick, Aaron Rodgers, Peyton Manning, Tom Brady, Russell Wilson, Michael Jordan, LeBron James, Kyrie Irving, Klay Thompson,*

Stephen Curry, Kevin Durant, Russell Westbrook, Anthony Davis, Chris Paul, Blake Griffin, Kobe Bryant, Joakim Noah, Scottie Pippen, Carmelo Anthony, Kevin Love, Grant Hill, Tracy McGrady, Vince Carter, Patrick Ewing, Karl Malone, Tony Parker, Allen Iverson, Hakeem Olajuwon, Reggie Miller, Michael Carter-Williams, John Wall, James Harden, Tim Duncan, Steve Nash, Draymond Green, Kawhi Leonard, Dwyane Wade, Ray Allen, Pau Gasol, Dirk Nowitzki, Jimmy Butler, Paul Pierce, Manu Ginobili, Pete Maravich, Larry Bird, Kyle Lowry, Jason Kidd, David Robinson, LaMarcus Aldridge, Derrick Rose, Paul George, Kevin Garnett, Chris Paul, Marc Gasol, Yao Ming, Al Horford, Amar'e Stoudemire, DeMar DeRozan, Isaiah Thomas, Kemba Walker and Chris Bosh in the Kindle Store. If you love basketball, check out my website at claytongeoffreys.com to join my exclusive list where I let you know about my latest books and give you lots of goodies.

Like what you read? Please leave a review!

I write because I love sharing the stories of influential athletes like Ben Simmons with fantastic readers like you. My readers inspire me to write more so please do not hesitate to let me know what you thought by leaving a review! If you love books on life, basketball, or productivity, check out my website at claytongeoffreys.com to join my exclusive list where I let you know about my latest books. Aside from being the first to hear about my latest releases, you can also download a free copy of *33 Life Lessons: Success Principles, Career Advice & Habits of Successful People*. See you there!

Clayton

References

i Woo, Jeremy. "LSU recruit Ben Simmons could be the next ambassador of Australian basketball". *Sports Illustrated*. 18 April 2014. Web.

ii Keeble, Brett. "Boomers boss sees something special in Simmons". *The Herald*. 29 October 2013. Web.

iii Arnovitz, Kevin. "You'll never believe the oblong ball behind Ben Simmons' genius". *ESPN*. 15 December 2017. Web.

iv Auerbach, Nicole. "LSU's versatile Ben Simmons has a natural position: Star". *USA Today*. 19 June 2015. Web.

v Bernard, Grantley. "This son of a gun has a very big future". *Herald Sun*. 24 November 2011. Web.

vi Borzello, Jeff. "Australian prospect Ben Simmons makes great first impression". *CBS Sports*. 8 June 2012. Web.

vii Goodman, Jeff. "No. 4 recruit Ben Simmons picks LSU". *ESPN*. 15 October 2013. Web.

viii "Ben Simmons the best all-round player since Lebron James: Magic Johnson". *ABC.net.au*. 6 January 2016. Web.

ix "Ben Simmons". *Draft Express*. Web.

x O'Connor, Kevin. "Ben Simmons scouting report". *NBC Sports*. 2016. Web.

xi "Ben Simmons scouting report compares him to LeBron James". *NJ.com*. 23 June 2016. Web.

xii Powell, Shaun. "Simmons ready to fulfil promise with fledgling Sixers". *NBA.com*. 10 July 2016. Web.

xiii Porter, Andrew. "Ben Simmons says he's gained 33 pounds of muscle". *CBS Philly*. 28 September 2016. Web.

xiv "Sixers say Ben Simons won't play this season; rookie 'heartbroken' over news.". *ESPN*. 24 February 2017. Web.

xv Jones, Gordie. "Examining how Markelle Fultz and Ben Simmons could mesh together on court". *NBC Sports*. 23 June 2017. Web.

xvi Hoffman, Benjamin. "Sixers guard Markelle Fultz out indefinitely with nerve disorder". *The New York Times*. 4 December 2018. Web.

xvii "Ben Simmons ready to make an impact in the NBA". *News.com.au*. 27 September 2017. Web.

xviii Begley, Ian. "Ben Simmons says 1-point performance was result of 'overthinking'". *ESPN*. 5 May 2018. Web.

xix Maloney, Jack. "76ers star Ben Simmons says improving jump shot has been main focus of his offseason training". *CBS Sports*. 29 August 2018. Web.

xx Smith, Jeff. "Ben Simmons is in ridiculous shape ahead of upcoming

season". *USA Today*. 28 August 2018. Web.
xxi Mutoni, Marcel. "Ben Simmons dismisses 'average' comment from Jared Dudley". *Slam Online*. 18 April 2019. Web.

Printed in Great Britain
by Amazon